Card Party

Size: **Card Box:** 6⅛ inches W x 1⅜ inches H x 4⅜ inches D (15.6cm x 3.5cm x 11.1cm)
Notepad Cover: Fits a 3 x 5-inch notepad (7.6cm x 12.7cm)
Snack Picks: Stitched motifs measure approximately 1–1⅛ inches square (2.5cm–2.9cm)
Skill Level: Beginner

Card Box
Design by Helen Miller

Materials

- ❑ 1 sheet clear 7-count plastic canvas
- ❑ Uniek Needloft plastic canvas yarn as listed in color key
- ❑ #16 tapestry needle

Stitching Step by Step

1 Cut one lid top, two lid sides and one box bottom from plastic canvas according to graphs (page 3).

2 Also cut two pieces 28 holes x 7 holes for lid ends; two pieces 38 holes x 7 holes for box sides; two pieces 26 holes x 7 holes for box ends; and one piece 25 holes x 7 holes for divider.

3 *Stitch lid:* Stitch lid top and lid sides according to graphs, filling in uncoded areas with white Continental Stitches. Fill lid ends with white Continental Stitches.

4 When background stitching is complete, Backstitch "Cards" on lid sides using black yarn.

5 *Stitch box:* Fill in uncoded box bottom with black Continental Stitches, leaving the rows marked in green unstitched for now. Box sides, ends and divider will remain unstitched.

Assembly

1 *Lid:* Whipstitch box lid sides and ends to lid using black yarn. Whipstitch sides and ends together along corners using white yarn. Overcast bottom edges of lid using Christmas red yarn.

2 *Box:* Referring to assembly diagram (page 2) throughout, Whipstitch unstitched box sides and ends together along corners using white yarn. Whipstitch assembled box sides and ends to box bottom along green lines using black yarn.

3 Overcast outer edge of box bottom using Christmas red yarn.

4 Whipstitch bottom edge of unstitched divider to box bottom along center green line using black yarn; Whipstitch ends of divider to adjacent rows of box sides using white yarn.

Notepad Cover
Design by Sandra Miller-Maxfield

Materials

- ❑ ¼ sheet clear 7-count plastic canvas
- ❑ Uniek Needloft plastic canvas yarn as listed in color key
- ❑ #16 tapestry needle
- ❑ 3 x 5-inch spiral-bound notepad
- ❑ Craft glue

Stitching Step by Step

1 Cut notepad cover from plastic canvas according to graph (page 4).

2 Stitch cover according to graph, filling in uncoded areas with white Continental Stitches. Overcast edges using black yarn.

3 When background stitching is complete, Straight Stitch a letter A in corners where indicated using black yarn.

4 Center and glue stitched cover to notepad cover.

Snack Picks

Designs by Sandra Miller-Maxfield

Materials

- ❑ Scraps of clear 10-count plastic canvas
- ❑ Uniek Needloft plastic canvas yarn as listed in color key
- ❑ #16 tapestry needle
- ❑ Wooden toothpicks or party picks
- ❑ Hot-glue gun

Stitching Step by Step

1 Cut club, spade, diamond and heart from plastic canvas according to graphs.

2 Fill club and spade with black Continental Stitches, Overcasting edges as you stitch. Fill diamond and heart with Christmas red Continental Stitches, Overcasting as you stitch.

3 Hot-glue end of toothpick to reverse side of stitched motif.

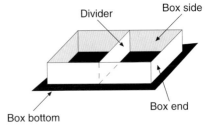

Card Box Assembly Diagram

Spade Snack Pick
11 holes x 12 holes
Cut 1

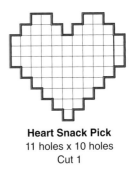

Heart Snack Pick
11 holes x 10 holes
Cut 1

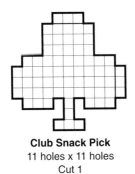

Club Snack Pick
11 holes x 11 holes
Cut 1

Diamond Snack Pick
9 holes x 11 holes
Cut 1

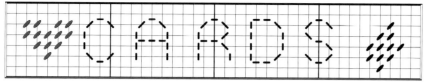

Card Box Lid Side
40 holes x 7 holes
Cut 2

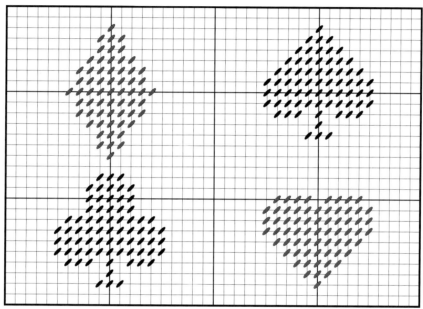

Card Box Lid Top
40 holes x 28 holes
Cut 1

COLOR KEY	
Yards	**Plastic Canvas Yarn**
32 (29.3m)	■ Black #00
12 (11m)	■ Christmas red #02
42 (38.5m)	Uncoded areas on box lid top, box lid side and notepad cover are white #41 Continental Stitches
	Uncoded areas on card box bottom, and club and spade snack picks are black #00 Continental Stitches
	Uncoded heart and diamond snack picks are Christmas red #02 Continental Stitches
	✒ Black #00 Backstitch and Straight Stitch

Color numbers given are for Uniek Needloft plastic canvas yarn.

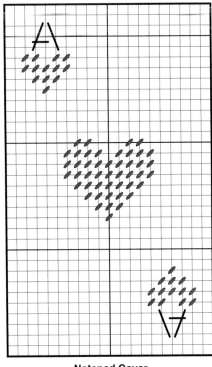

Notepad Cover
20 holes x 33 holes
Cut 1

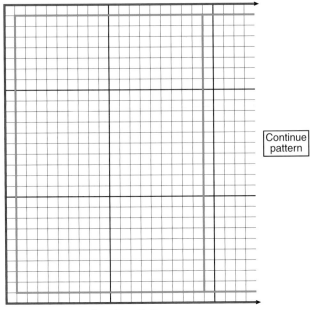

Continue pattern

Card Box Bottom
40 holes x 28 holes
Cut 1

COLOR KEY

Yards	Plastic Canvas Yarn
32 (29.3m)	■ Black #00
12 (11m)	■ Christmas red #02
42 (38.5m)	Uncoded areas on box lid top, box lid side and notepad cover are white #41 Continental Stitches
	Uncoded areas on card box bottom, and club and spade snack picks are black #00 Continental Stitches
	Uncoded heart and diamond snack picks are Christmas red #02 Continental Stitches
	╱ Black #00 Backstitch and Straight Stitch

Color numbers given are for Uniek Needloft plastic canvas yarn.

Dominoes

Design by Patsy Brusuelas

Size: **Case:** 9½ inches W x 1¼ inches H x
5 inches D (24.1cm x 3.2cm x 12.7cm)
Dominoes: 2¼ inches W x 1¼ inches W x
⅜ inch D (5.7cm x 3.2cm x 1 cm)

Skill Level: Beginner

Materials

- ❑ 2 sheets clear 7-count plastic canvas
- ❑ Uniek Needloft plastic canvas yarn as listed in color key
- ❑ Uniek Needloft craft cord as listed in color key
- ❑ #16 tapestry needle
- ❑ 5 small self-adhesive hook-and-loop closures
- ❑ Hot-glue gun

Stitching Step by Step

Dominoes

1 Cut one of each domino, 1–28, from plastic canvas according to graphs (pages 6 and 7).

2 Also cut 28 pieces 7 x 14 holes to serve as bottoms of dominoes; 56 strips 14 holes x 2 holes for domino sides; and 56 strips 7 holes x 2 holes for domino ends.

3 Stitch dominoes according to graphs. Stitch domino bottoms in same background pattern using all black yarn and omitting markings. Work black Continental Stitches down centers of all domino side strips and end strips.

4 *Assemble domino:* Using black yarn throughout, Whipstitch two domino sides and two domino ends to matching edges of a stitched domino. Whipstitch sides and ends together at corners. Whipstitch black domino bottom to remaining edges to complete domino. Repeat to assemble all dominos.

Case

1 Cut one case lid, two case flaps and three dominoes of your choice from plastic canvas according to graphs (page 8).

2 Also cut one piece 61 holes x 8 holes for case lid front flap; one piece 61 holes x 33 holes for case bottom; two pieces 61 holes x 7 holes for case sides; and two pieces 33 holes x 7 holes for case ends.

3 Stitch dominoes, case lid and case flaps according to graphs, Overcasting dominos as you stitch. Fill in remaining plastic canvas pieces *except case bottom* with vertical rows of royal Slanted Gobelin Stitches in same pattern as lid and case flaps. Case bottom will remain unstitched.

4 *Assemble case:* Using royal yarn and referring to assembly diagram (page 8) throughout, Whipstitch case sides and ends to edges of case bottom. Whipstitch case sides and ends together at corners. Whipstitch edges of case flaps to top edges of case ends between arrows; flaps will fold in over dominoes.

5 *Attach lid:* Whipstitch case lid front flap to front edge of lid. Whipstitch back edge of lid to top edge of case side on back of case.

6 Overcast all unfinished edges.

7 Affix hook-and-loop closures to case, lid and flaps where indicated by white rectangles on assembly diagram.

8 Arrange three extra dominoes on lid as desired and hot-glue in place. Place 1–28 dominoes in completed case.

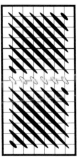

Domino Top 1
7 holes x 14 holes
Cut 1

Domino Top 2
7 holes x 14 holes
Cut 1

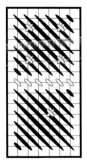

Domino Top 3
7 holes x 14 holes
Cut 1

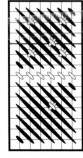

Domino Top 4
7 holes x 14 holes
Cut 1

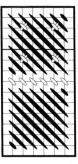

Domino Top 5
7 holes x 14 holes
Cut 1

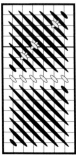

Domino Top 6
7 holes x 14 holes
Cut 1

Domino Top 7
7 holes x 14 holes
Cut 1

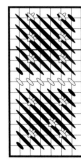

Domino Top 8
7 holes x 14 holes
Cut 1

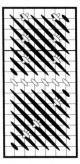

Domino Top 9
7 holes x 14 holes
Cut 1

Domino Top 10
7 holes x 14 holes
Cut 1

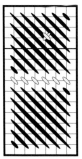

Domino Top 11
7 holes x 14 holes
Cut 1

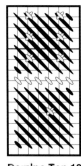

Domino Top 12
7 holes x 14 holes
Cut 1

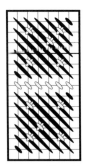

Domino Top 13
7 holes x 14 holes
Cut 1

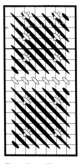

Domino Top 14
7 holes x 14 holes
Cut 1

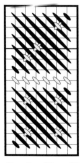

Domino Top 15
7 holes x 14 holes
Cut 1

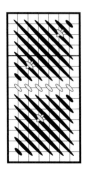

Domino Top 16
7 holes x 14 holes
Cut 1

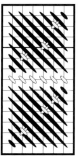

Domino Top 17
7 holes x 14 holes
Cut 1

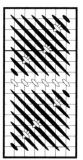

Domino Top 18
7 holes x 14 holes
Cut 1

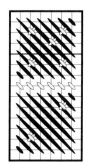

Domino Top 19
7 holes x 14 holes
Cut 1

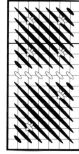

Domino Top 20
7 holes x 14 holes
Cut 1

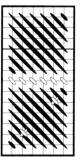

Domino Top 21
7 holes x 14 holes
Cut 1

Domino Top 22
7 holes x 14 holes
Cut 1

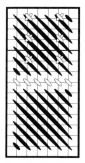

Domino Top 23
7 holes x 14 holes
Cut 1

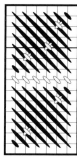

Domino Top 24
7 holes x 14 holes
Cut 1

Domino Top 25
7 holes x 14 holes
Cut 1

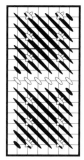

Domino Top 26
7 holes x 14 holes
Cut 1

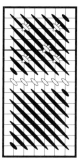

Domino Top 27
7 holes x 14 holes
Cut 1

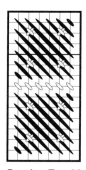

Domino Top 28
7 holes x 14 holes
Cut 1

COLOR KEY

Yards	Plastic Canvas Yarn
87 (79.6m)	■ Black #00
58 (53.1m)	■ Royal #32
18 (16.5m)	□ White #41
	Craft Cord
3 (2.8m)	■ Iridescent white #55033

Color numbers given are for Uniek Needloft
plastic canvas yarn and craft cord.

Back Edge

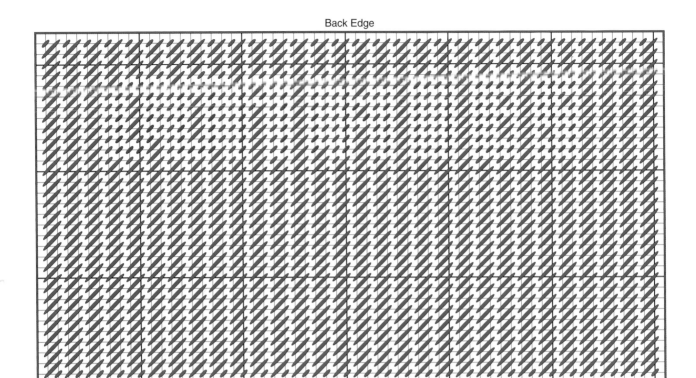

Front Edge

Dominoes Case Lid
61 holes x 33 holes
Cut 1

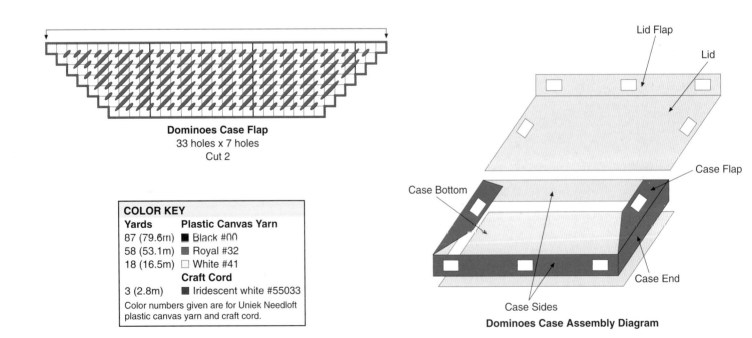

Dominoes Case Flap
33 holes x 7 holes
Cut 2

COLOR KEY

Yards	Plastic Canvas Yarn
87 (79.6m)	■ Black #00
58 (53.1m)	■ Royal #32
18 (16.5m)	☐ White #41
	Craft Cord
3 (2.8m)	■ Iridescent white #55033

Color numbers given are for Uniek Needloft plastic canvas yarn and craft cord.

Dominoes Case Assembly Diagram

Lid Flap
Lid
Case Flap
Case Bottom
Case End
Case Sides

Horseshoes

Design by Trudy Bath Smith

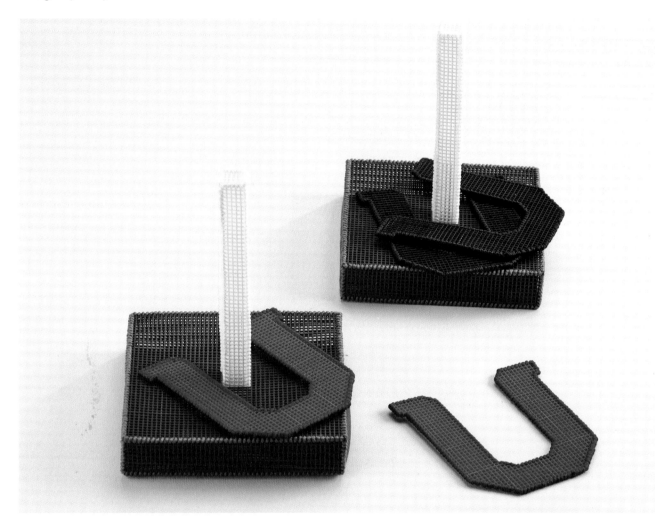

Size: **Box:** 7⅜ inches W x 1½ inches H x
7⅜ inches D (18.7cm x 3.8cm x 18.7cm)
Stake: ⅞ inch square x 9 inches H
(2.2cm x 22.9cm)
Horseshoe: 5¾ inches W x 6⅛ inches H
(14.6cm x 15.6cm)

Skill Level: Beginner

Materials

❑ 7-count plastic canvas:
   2 sheets green
   1½ sheets black
   1½ sheets red
   ½ sheet white
❑ Uniek Needloft plastic canvas yarn as
   listed in color key
❑ #16 tapestry needle
❑ 2 self-adhesive hook-and-loop closures

Stitching Step by Step

Boxes

Cut all pieces from green plastic canvas and work all stitching with Christmas green yarn.

1 *For each box,* cut two box top/bottom pieces according to graph (page 12), cutting center opening from one piece only.

2 *For each box,* also cut four pieces 48 holes x 9 holes for box sides; four 7-hole x 2-hole strips for stake stabilizers; and one piece 8 holes x 9 holes for closure tab.

3 Top/bottom piece with cutout opening serves as box bottom. *Do not Overcast cutout opening.* Whipstitch box sides to edges of box bottom; Whipstitch sides together along corners.

4 Whipstitch stake stabilizer strips together along their ends to form a shallow square. Whipstitch square to center of box top (without opening) where indicated by green lines in center of graph, matching position of cutout opening in the box bottom.

5 Whipstitch 8-hole edge of closure tab to center of one edge of box top. Whipstitch opposite edge of box top to top edge of one box side so that stake stabilizer strips are *inside* box when box is closed.

6 Affix halves of hook-and-loop closure to closure tab and box side.

7 Repeat to make a second box.

Stakes

Cut pieces from white plastic canvas and work all stitching with white yarn.

1 *For each stake,* cut four pieces 59 holes x 5 holes for stake sides and two pieces 5 holes x 5 holes for stake ends.

2 Whipstitch sides together along long edges to form a long, square column. Whipstitch ends to ends of stake.

3 Repeat to make a second stake.

Horseshoes

1 Cut four horseshoes from red plastic canvas according to graph; do not stitch.

2 Holding horseshoes together in pairs, Whipstitch edges using red yarn.

3 Repeat steps 1 and 2, substituting black plastic canvas and black yarn.

Playing & Storage

To play, turn closed boxes upside down, with opening on top. Insert stakes, seating the end inside stabilizer strips inside box. Toss horseshoes at stakes.

Store a stake and two horseshoes in each box.

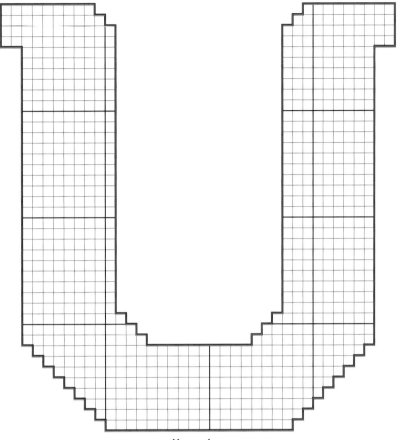

Horseshoe
38 holes x 40 holes
Cut 4 from red and 4 from black
Whipstitch red horseshoes as shown;
substitute black yarn on black horseshoes

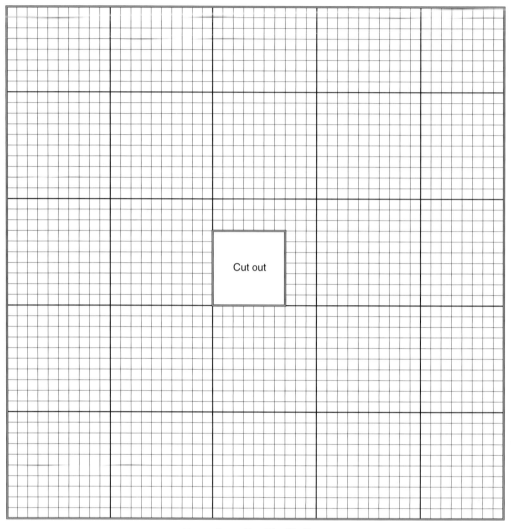

Horseshoes Box Top/Bottom
48 holes x 48 holes
Cut 4 from green,
cutting opening from 2 only

COLOR KEY	
Yards	**Plastic Canvas Yarn**
5 (4.6m)	✏ Black #00 Whipstitch
5 (4.6m)	✏ Red #01 Whipstitch
6 (5.5m)	✏ Christmas green #28 Whipstitch
5 (4.6m)	✏ White #41 Whipstitch
Color numbers given are for Uniek Needloft plastic canvas yarn.	

Tic-Tac-Toe

Designs by Vicki Blizzard

Size: **Box:** 4⅝ inches square x 2 inches H
(11.8cm x 5.1cm)
Playing Pieces: vary in size from ⅞–2 inches W
x 1½–2¾ inches H (2.3–5.1cm x 3.8–7cm)
Skill Level: Beginner

Materials

For each set:

❑ 1 sheet clear 7-count plastic canvas
❑ Uniek Needloft plastic canvas yarn as
   listed in color key
❑ 6-strand embroidery floss as listed in color key
❑ #16 tapestry needle

Stitching Step by Step

Bears & Hearts

Box/Playing Board

1 Cut one lid top from plastic canvas according to graph (page 15), carefully cutting away shaded gray areas.

2 Also cut four pieces 30 holes x 5 holes for lid sides; one piece 28 holes x 28 holes for box bottom; and four pieces 28 holes x 11 holes for box sides.

3 Stitch lid top according to graph, filling in uncoded areas with eggshell Continental Stitches and Overcasting cutout openings with eggshell as you stitch. Fill lid sides and box sides with eggshell Continental Stitches; box bottom will remain unstitched.

4 Using pink yarn throughout, Whipstitch lid sides to edges of lid top; Whipstitch lid sides together at corners. Referring to stitch diagrams (page 15), Overcast bottom edge of lid using Herringbone Overcast Stitch.

5 Using eggshell yarn throughout, Whipstitch box sides to edges of box bottom; Whipstitch box sides together at corners and Overcast top edge of box. Store playing pieces in box when not in use.

Playing Pieces

1 Cut 10 bears and 10 hearts from plastic canvas according to graphs (page 14).

2 Using pink yarn throughout, fill uncoded hearts with pink Continental Stitches. Whipstitch hearts together in pairs to make five playing pieces.

3 Stitch five bears according to graph for fronts, filling uncoded areas with cinnamon Continental Stitches; fill remaining bears with cinnamon Continental Stitches for backs.

4 *When background stitching is complete, embroider bear fronts using 6 plies black embroidery floss:* Backstitch and Straight Stitch mouths. Work French Knot eyes, wrapping floss twice around needle. Work French Knot noses, wrapping floss once around needle.

5 Using cinnamon yarn, Whipstitch bear fronts and backs together in pairs to make five playing pieces.

Cars & Traffic Lights

Box/Playing Board

Follow instructions for making Box/Playing Board for Bears & Hearts game, substituting black yarn for eggshell and white yarn for pink.

Playing Pieces

1 Cut 10 cars and 10 traffic lights from plastic canvas according to graphs.

2 Stitch five cars according to graph for fronts; fill remaining cars with royal Continental Stitches for backs.

3 When background stitching is complete, Backstitch windows and doors on fronts using 6 plies black embroidery floss.

4 Using royal and black yarn according to graph, Whipstitch car fronts and backs together in pairs to make five playing pieces.

5 Stitch five traffic lights according to graph for fronts, working Christmas red, yellow and fern Smyrna Cross Stitches for lights last; fill remaining lights with yellow Continental Stitches for backs.

6 Using yellow yarn, Whipstitch traffic light fronts and backs together in pairs to make five playing pieces.

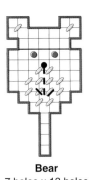

Bear
7 holes x 13 holes
Cut 10
Stitch 5 as shown for fronts;
stitch 5 in cinnamon for backs

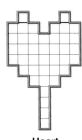

Heart
7 holes x 11 holes
Cut 10

COLOR KEY	
BEARS & HEARTS	
Yards	**Plastic Canvas Yarn**
35 (32.1m)	■ Pink #07
42 (38.5m)	☐ Eggshell #39
15 (13.8m)	Uncoded areas on bear are cinnamon #14 Continental Stitches
	Uncoded hearts are pink #07 Continental Stitches
	Uncoded areas on lid are eggshell #39 Continental Stitches
	⁄ Cinnamon #14 Whipstitch
	6-Strand Embroidery Floss
2 (1.9m)	⁄ Black Backstitch and Straight Stitch
	● Black (1-wrap) French Knot
	● Black (2-wrap) French Knot
Color numbers given are for Uniek Needloft plastic canvas yarn.	

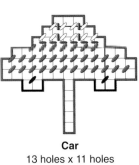

Car
13 holes x 11 holes
Cut 10
Stitch 5 as shown for fronts;
stitch 5 in royal for backs

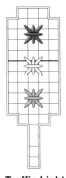

Traffic Light
5 holes x 15 holes
Cut 10
Stitch 5 as shown for fronts;
stitch 5 in yellow for backs

COLOR KEY	
CARS & TRAFFIC LIGHTS	
Yards	**Plastic Canvas Yarn**
46 (42.1m)	■ Black #00
14 (12.9m)	■ Royal #32
24 (22m)	☐ White #41
	Uncoded areas on lid are black #00 Continental Stitches
	Uncoded areas on traffic light are yellow #57 Continental Stitches
1 (1m)	✳ Christmas red #02 Smyrna Cross Stitch
1 (1m)	✳ Fern #23 Smyrna Cross Stitch
15 (13.8m)	✳ Yellow #57 Smyrna Cross Stitch
	⁄ Yellow #57 Whipstitch
	6-Strand Embroidery Floss
3 (2.8m)	⁄ Black Backstitch
Color numbers given are for Uniek Needloft plastic canvas yarn.	

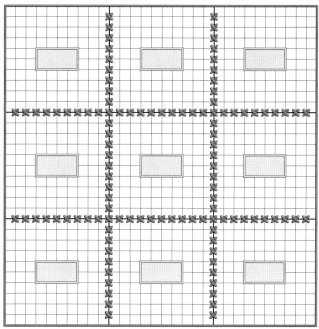

Tic-Tac-Toe Lid Top
30 holes x 30 holes
Cut 1 for each game, cutting away gray areas
Stitch as shown for Bears & Hearts;
substitute white for pink and black for eggshell for Cars & Traffic Lights

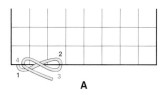

A

Bring needle up at 1, over
the edge and down behind
canvas at 2, up at 3,
then over the edge and
down behind canvas at 4.

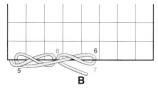

B

Bring needle around
edge and up at 5,
down behind canvas at 6,
up at 7 and down behind
canvas at 8.

Herringbone Overcast Stitch

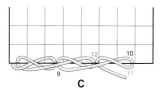

C

Bring needle under edge, around
yarn and up at 9, down at 10,
up at 11 and down at 12.
Continue until edge is covered.

Fun with Darts

Design by Maria Berenger

Size: 12¼ inches W x 14 inches H x 2 inches D
(31.1cm x 35.6cm x 5.1cm)
Skill Level: Beginner

Materials

❑ 5 artist-size sheets clear stiff 7-count plastic canvas
❑ Uniek Needloft plastic canvas yarn as listed
   in color key
❑ 2 (½-inch/13mm) plastic rings
❑ 11¾-inch-square x 1½-inch-thick sheet
   of plastic foam
❑ 3 table tennis balls
❑ ½-inch (13mm) hook-and-loop circles:
   18 each black, red and tan
❑ #16 tapestry needle
❑ Sewing needle and thread
❑ Craft glue or hot-glue gun

Stitching Step by Step

Cutting & Stitching

1 Cut one dartboard front, four doors, one back and two sides from plastic canvas according to graphs (pages 17–21).

2 Also cut three strips 80 holes x 12 holes for dartboard top, dartboard bottom and dartboard case bottom.

3 Stitch dartboard front and doors according to graphs, filling in uncoded areas with gray Continental Stitches.

4 When background stitching is complete, Backstitch numerals onto dartboard front using 2 plies separated from a strand of white yarn.

5 Stitch bottom 11 rows of back with gray Continental Stitches as shown, leaving remainder of back unstitched.

6 Fill in one uncoded dartboard side with gray Continental Stitches, leaving the row indicated by red line unstitched for now. Stitch the second dartboard side in the same manner, reversing the position of the unstitched row.

7 Fill in one 80-hole x 12-hole strip with gray Continental Stitches for dartboard top; strips for dartboard bottom and dartboard case bottom will remain unstitched.

Assembly

1 Referring to assembly diagram Fig. 1 (page 21), lay stitched dartboard back right side up. Using gray yarn throughout, Whipstitch stitched dartboard top along top edge; Whipstitch sides to side edges of back with unstitched rows indicated by red lines positioned at front.

2 Whipstitch unstitched dartboard bottom strip to back where indicated by red line on back graph; *do not* Whipstitch ends of bottom to sides.

3 Whipstitch unstitched dartboard case bottom to bottom edge of back.

4 Fold up dartboard top, side and case bottom strips to form a shallow box; Whipstitch together along corners.

5 *Hangers:* Using needle and thread, stitch plastic rings on reverse side of case near top corners.

6 Insert plastic foam in case.

7 Referring to Fig. 2 (page 21) throughout, lay stitched dartboard front over plastic foam. Using gray yarn,

Whipstitch side edges to dartboard sides along unstitched rows indicated by red line on graph. Using black yarn, Whipstitch dartboard front to case along top edge and along front edge of unstitched dartboard bottom strip.

8 Hold stitched doors together in pairs, wrong sides facing; using black yarn throughout, Whipstitch pairs along top and bottom edges and one side edge. Whipstitch unfinished edges of doors to unfinished side edges of dartboard case, working through all layers.

9 Using black yarn, Overcast remaining unfinished edges.

Ball "Darts"

1 Glue hook portions of all black hook-and-loop dots to one table tennis ball as shown.

2 Repeat, gluing red and tan dots to remaining balls.

3 Use balls as "darts." When not in use, store balls in bottom shelf of dartboard case. Doors may be closed or left open as desired.

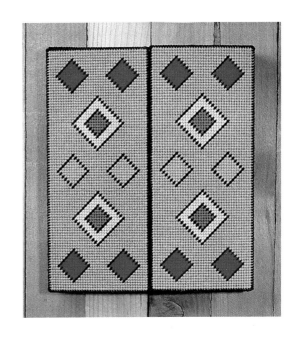

COLOR KEY

Yards	Plastic Canvas Yarn
88 (80.5m)	■ Black #00
20 (18.3m)	■ Red #01
14 (12.9m)	■ Holly #27
34 (31.1m)	□ Silver #37
270 (246.9m)	■ Gray #38
17 (15.6m)	□ White #41
17 (15.6m)	■ Camel #43

Uncoded areas are gray #38 Continental Stitches

⁄⁄ White #41 (2-ply) Backstitch

Color numbers given are for Uniek Needloft plastic canvas yarn.

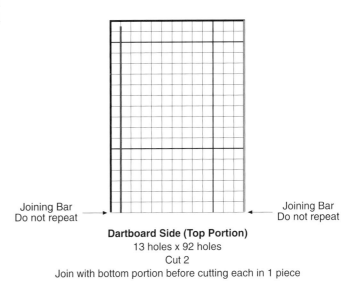

Joining Bar Do not repeat → ← Joining Bar Do not repeat

Dartboard Side (Top Portion)
13 holes x 92 holes
Cut 2
Join with bottom portion before cutting each in 1 piece

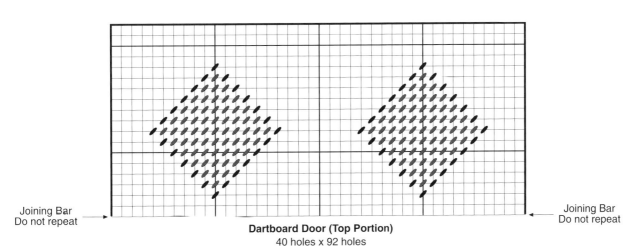

Joining Bar Do not repeat → ← Joining Bar Do not repeat

Dartboard Door (Top Portion)
40 holes x 92 holes
Cut 4
Join with bottom portion before cutting each in 1 piece

Joining Bar
Do not repeat →

← Joining Bar
Do not repeat

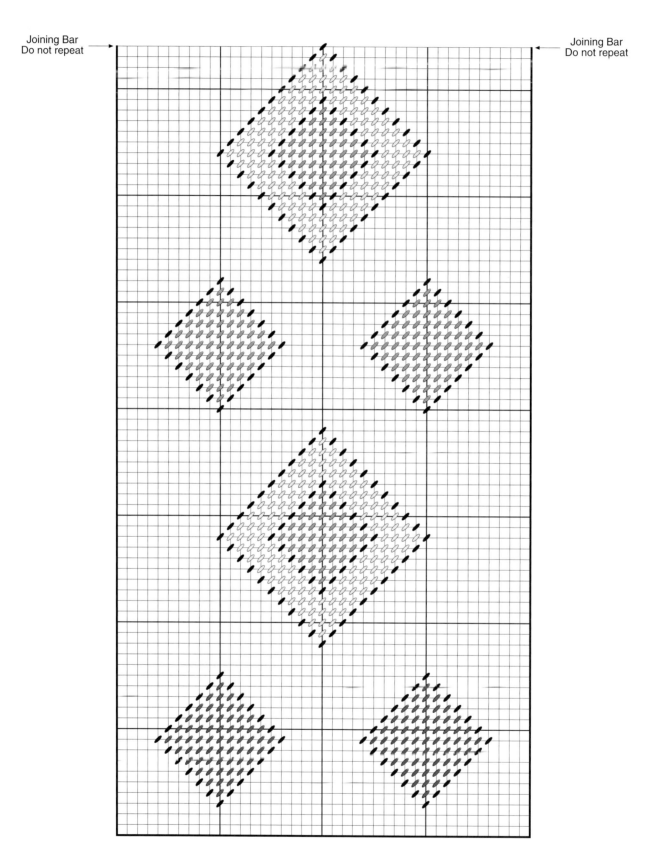

Dartboard Door (Bottom Portion)
40 holes x 92 holes
Cut 4
Join with top portion before cutting each in 1 piece

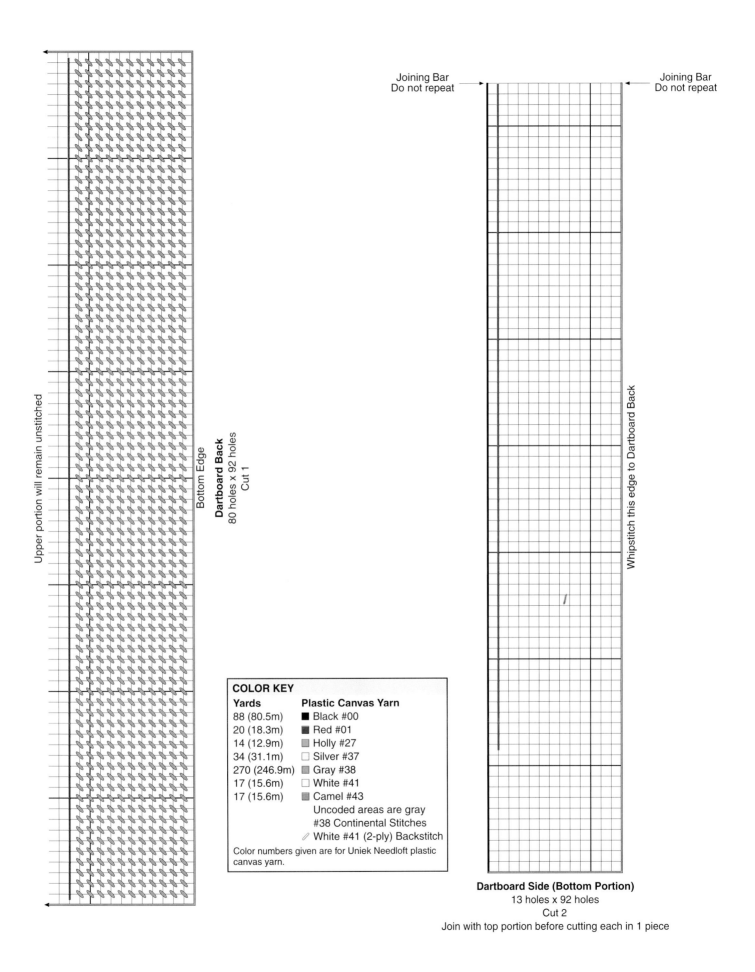

Upper portion will remain unstitched

Bottom Edge

Dartboard Back
80 holes x 92 holes
Cut 1

Joining Bar
Do not repeat

Joining Bar
Do not repeat

Whipstitch this edge to Dartboard Back

COLOR KEY

Yards	Plastic Canvas Yarn
88 (80.5m)	■ Black #00
20 (18.3m)	■ Red #01
14 (12.9m)	▨ Holly #27
34 (31.1m)	☐ Silver #37
270 (246.9m)	▨ Gray #38
17 (15.6m)	☐ White #41
17 (15.6m)	▨ Camel #43

Uncoded areas are gray
#38 Continental Stitches
⁄ White #41 (2-ply) Backstitch

Color numbers given are for Uniek Needloft plastic
canvas yarn.

Dartboard Side (Bottom Portion)
13 holes x 92 holes
Cut 2
Join with top portion before cutting each in 1 piece

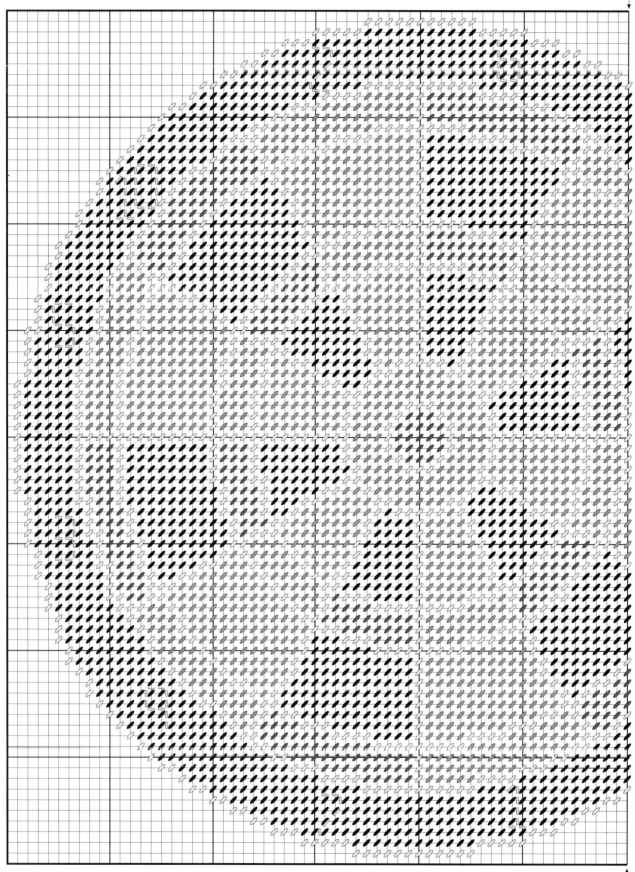

Dartboard Front (Left Portion)
80 holes x 80 holes
Cut 1
Join with right portion before cutting in 1 piece

Joining Bar
Do not repeat

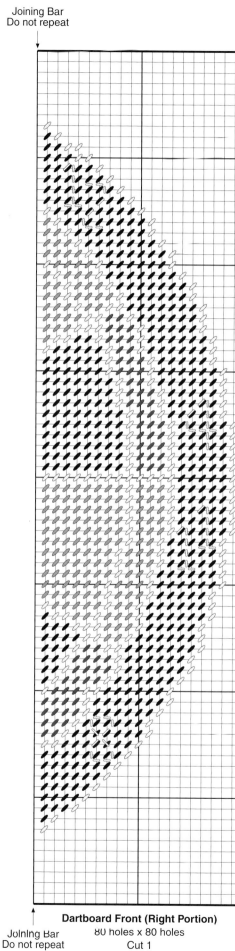

Dartboard Front (Right Portion)
80 holes x 80 holes
Cut 1
Join with left portion before
cutting in 1 piece

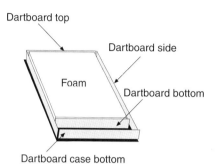

Dartboard top

Dartboard side

Foam

Dartboard bottom

Dartboard case bottom

Fig. 1

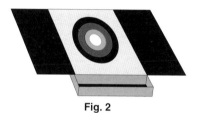

Fig. 2

Dartboard Assembly Diagrams

COLOR KEY	
Yards	**Plastic Canvas Yarn**
88 (80.5m)	■ Black #00
20 (18.3m)	■ Red #01
14 (12.9m)	▨ Holly #27
34 (31.1m)	☐ Silver #37
270 (246.9m)	▨ Gray #38
17 (15.6m)	☐ White #41
17 (15.6m)	▨ Camel #43

Uncoded areas are gray
#38 Continental Stitches
⟋ White #41 (2-ply) Backstitch

Color numbers given are for Uniek Needloft plastic
canvas yarn.

Primary Shape Sorter

Design by Cindy M. Gober

Size: 6¾ inches square x 12⅝ inches H
(17.1cm x 32.1cm)
Skill Level: Beginner

Materials

❏ 7-count plastic canvas:
   3 artist-size sheets clear stiff
   1 regular sheet dark blue
   1 regular sheet dark green
   1 regular sheet purple
   1 regular sheet red
❏ Uniek Needloft plastic canvas yarn as
   listed in color key
❏ #16 tapestry needle

Stitching Step by Step

Shapes

Use yarn color to match plastic canvas color throughout.

1 *Circles:* Cut two circles each from blue, green, purple and red plastic canvas according to graph. Also cut one strip 38 holes x 10 holes from each color for circle sides. Bend each strip into a ring; Whipstitch ends. Whipstitch circles to edges.

2 *Triangles:* Cut two triangles each from blue, green, purple and red plastic canvas according to graph. Also cut three strips 17 holes x 5 holes from each color for triangle sides. Whipstitch ends of matching strips together to form triangular frame. Whipstitch triangles to edges.

3 *Squares:* Cut six 10-hole x 10-hole squares each from blue, green, purple and red plastic canvas. Whipstitch matching squares together to form cubes.

4 *Rectangles:* Cut two 10-hole x 15-hole rectangles each from blue, green, purple and red plastic canvas. Also cut two strips 15 holes x 5 holes; and two strips 10 holes x 5 holes from each color for rectangle sides. Whipstitch ends of matching 5-hole wide strips together to form rectangular frames. Whipstitch rectangles to edges.

Sorter House

Cut all pieces from clear stiff plastic canvas.

1 Cut two front/back pieces according to graph (page 24), cutting openings from one piece only for front. Cut two handles and two roof pieces from plastic canvas according to graphs.

2 Also cut two pieces 44 holes x 46 holes for sides; one piece 44 holes x 44 holes for bottom; and one strip 2 holes x 44 holes for roof support. Bottom and roof support will remain unstitched.

3 Stitch front in red, Overcasting cutout openings as you stitch. Stitch back in Christmas green.

4 Stitch one roof piece in red and the second in Christmas green.

5 Using the same pattern of Slanted Gobelin Stitches worked in horizontal rows, stitch one side in royal and the other side in purple.

6 Stitch handles according to graph, Overcasting inner and outer edges as you stitch, but leaving ends between arrows unstitched for now.

7 *Assemble sorter house:* Using red yarn and referring to photo throughout, Whipstitch house front to sides. Using Christmas green yarn, Whipstitch back to sides. Using adjacent colors, Whipstitch bottom to assembled front, back and sides.

8 *Roof support:* Using red yarn, Whipstitch end of roof support to peak at top of front where indicated by arrows on front/back graph. Overcast remaining edges along top of front wall. Using Christmas green yarn, repeat to attach other end of roof support to back wall and finish top edge of back wall.

9 *Roof:* Center handles along top edges of roof pieces. Whipstitch handle ends to roof pieces using Christmas green yarn on Christmas green roof and red yarn on red roof. Center Christmas green roof along top edge of royal wall and red roof along top edge of purple wall. Using yarn color to match roof, Whipstitch roof pieces to walls; Overcast unfinished roof edges.

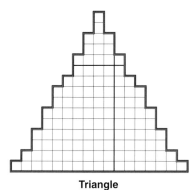

Triangle
17 holes x 15 holes
Cut 2 each from purple, red, green and blue
Whipstitch using matching colors

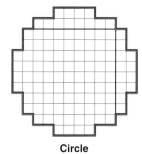

Circle
12 holes x 12 holes
Cut 2 each from purple, red, green and blue
Whipstitch using matching colors

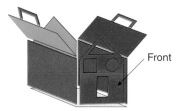

Shape Sorter Assembly Diagram

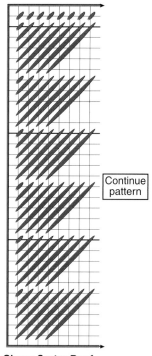

Continue pattern

Shape Sorter Roof
48 holes x 32 holes
Cut 2 from clear stiff
Stitch 1 as shown; stitch 1 in green

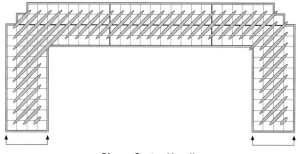

Shape Sorter Handle
28 holes x 12 holes
Cut 2 from clear stiff

COLOR KEY	
Yards	**Plastic Canvas Yarn**
70 (64m)	■ Red #01
72 (65.8m)	Christmas green #28
38 (34.7m)	▨ Royal #32
38 (34.7m)	Purple #46
Color numbers given are for Uniek Needloft plastic canvas yarn.	

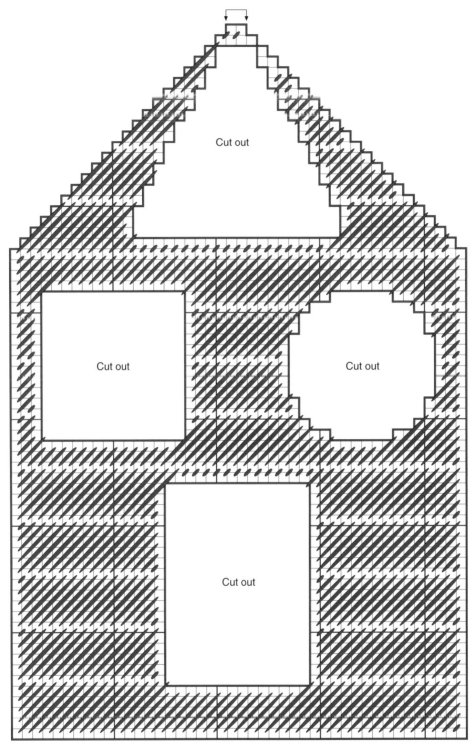

Cut out

Cut out

Cut out

Cut out

Shape Sorter Front/Back
44 holes x 67 holes
Cut 2 from clear stiff, cutting openings from front only
Stitch front as shown;
stitch back in Christmas green

COLOR KEY	
Yards	**Plastic Canvas Yarn**
70 (64m)	■ Red #01
72 (65.8m)	Christmas green #28
38 (34.7m)	▨ Royal #32
38 (34.7m)	Purple #46
Color numbers given are for Uniek Needloft plastic canvas yarn.	

Make a Face

Design by Terry Ricioli

Size: Face measures approximately 7¼ inches W x 10½ inches H (18.4cm x 26.7cm)

Skill Level: Beginner

Materials

❑ 3 sheets clear 7-count plastic canvas
❑ Medium weight yarn as listed in color key
❑ #16 tapestry needle
❑ Temporary-bond adhesive

Stitching Step by Step

1 Cut face, ears, noses, eyes and other facial features and accessories from plastic canvas according to graphs (pages 26–31).

2 *Clown hair:* Before stitching clown hair, reverse one piece. Referring to stitch diagram (page 30), fill clown hair pieces with orange Turkey Loop Stitches, making loops ¾ inch (1.9cm) long.

3 *Girl's hair:* Stitch girl's hair and Overcast according to graph (page 28). Cut 20 (12-inch/30.5cm) strands of yellow yarn; thread two strands through each hole indicated by a black dot on graph. Braid strands or leave them hanging loose as desired.

4 *Ear and eyebrow B:* Reverse one of each before stitching and Overcasting according to graphs (page 28).

5 Stitch and Overcast remaining pieces according to graphs.

6 Apply temporary adhesive to the reverse side of stitched facial features and accessories. Press features onto face to create a variety of faces.

Storage Tip: *When not in use, press adhesive-backed pieces onto a spare piece of lint-free fabric or another sheet of plastic canvas.*

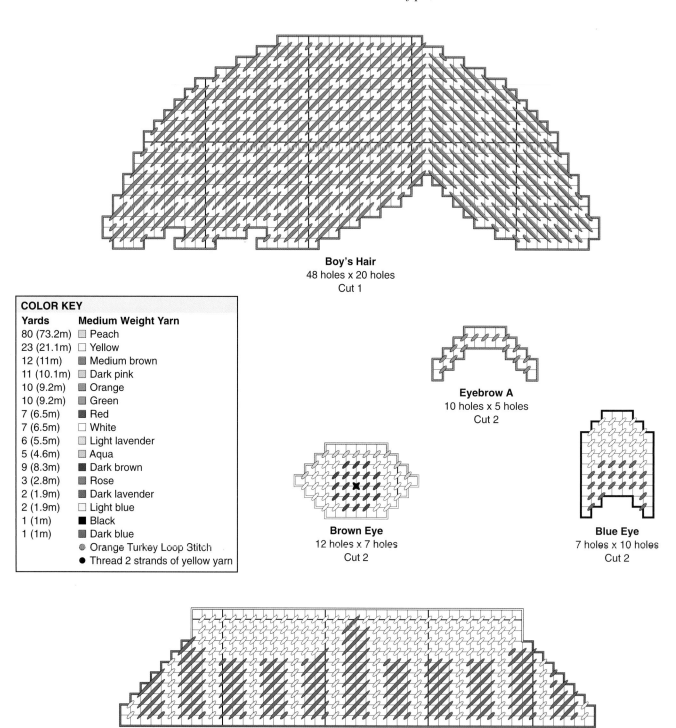

Boy's Hair
48 holes x 20 holes
Cut 1

COLOR KEY

Yards	Medium Weight Yarn
80 (73.2m)	Peach
23 (21.1m)	Yellow
12 (11m)	Medium brown
11 (10.1m)	Dark pink
10 (9.2m)	Orange
10 (9.2m)	Green
7 (6.5m)	Red
7 (6.5m)	White
6 (5.5m)	Light lavender
5 (4.6m)	Aqua
9 (8.3m)	Dark brown
3 (2.8m)	Rose
2 (1.9m)	Dark lavender
2 (1.9m)	Light blue
1 (1m)	Black
1 (1m)	Dark blue
	Orange Turkey Loop Stitch
	Thread 2 strands of yellow yarn

Eyebrow A
10 holes x 5 holes
Cut 2

Brown Eye
12 holes x 7 holes
Cut 2

Blue Eye
7 holes x 10 holes
Cut 2

Boy's Collar
46 holes x 11 holes
Cut 1

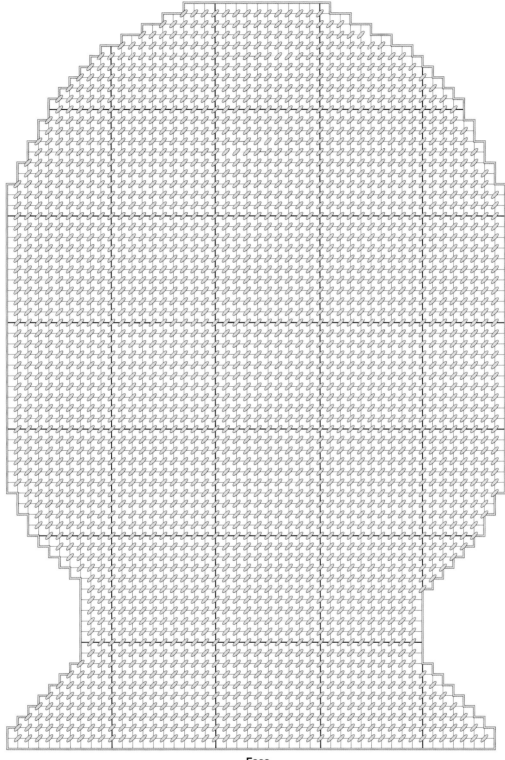

Face
48 holes x 70 holes
Cut 1

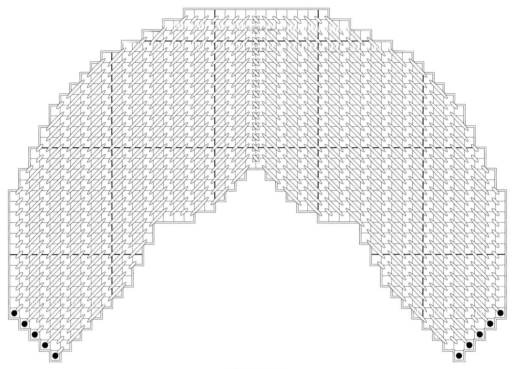

Girl's Hair
48 holes x 33 holes
Cut 1

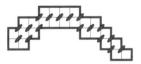

Eyebrow B
12 holes x 5 holes
Cut 2, reverse 1
before stitching

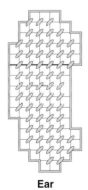

Ear
7 holes x 15 holes
Cut 2, reverse 1
before stitching

COLOR KEY	
Yards	**Medium Weight Yarn**
80 (73.2m)	Peach
23 (21.1m)	Yellow
12 (11m)	Medium brown
11 (10.1m)	Dark pink
10 (9.2m)	Orange
10 (9.2m)	Green
7 (6.5m)	Red
7 (6.5m)	White
6 (5.5m)	Light lavender
5 (4.6m)	Aqua
9 (8.3m)	Dark brown
3 (2.8m)	Rose
2 (1.9m)	Dark lavender
2 (1.9m)	Light blue
1 (1m)	Black
1 (1m)	Dark blue
	● Orange Turkey Loop Stitch
	● Thread 2 strands of yellow yarn

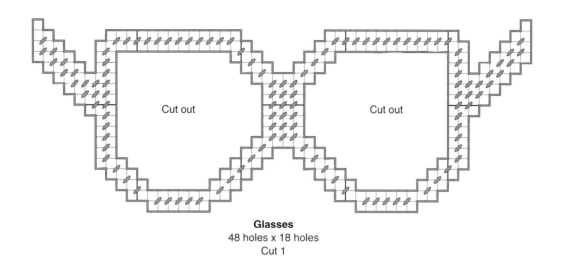

Glasses
48 holes x 18 holes
Cut 1

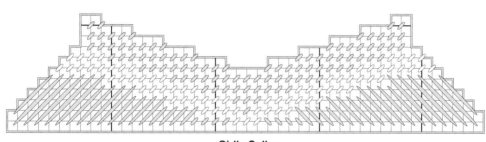

Girl's Collar
46 holes x 11 holes
Cut 1

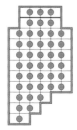

Clown Hair
6 holes x 11 holes
Cut 2, reverse 1 before stitching

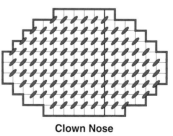

Clown Nose
16 holes x 10 holes
Cut 1

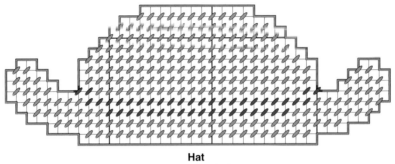

Hat
37 holes x 13 holes
Cut 1

Large Bow
31 holes x 15 holes
Cut 1

COLOR KEY

Yards	Medium Weight Yarn
80 (73.2m)	Peach
23 (21.1m)	Yellow
12 (11m)	Medium brown
11 (10.1m)	Dark pink
10 (9.2m)	Orange
10 (9.2m)	Green
7 (6.5m)	Red
7 (6.5m)	White
6 (5.5m)	Light lavender
5 (4.6m)	Aqua
9 (8.3m)	Dark brown
3 (2.8m)	Rose
2 (1.9m)	Dark lavender
2 (1.9m)	Light blue
1 (1m)	Black
1 (1m)	Dark blue
	Orange Turkey Loop Stitch
	Thread 2 strands of yellow yarn

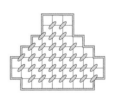

Small Nose
9 holes x 7 holes
Cut 1

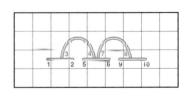

Turkey Loop Stitch

Mustache
45 holes x 11 holes
Cut 1

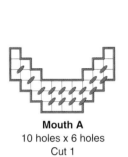

Mouth A
10 holes x 6 holes
Cut 1

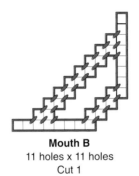

Mouth B
11 holes x 11 holes
Cut 1

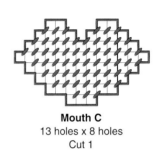

Mouth C
13 holes x 8 holes
Cut 1

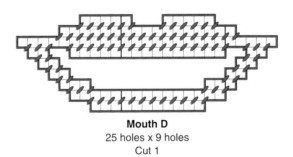

Mouth D
25 holes x 9 holes
Cut 1

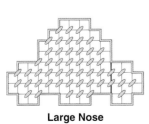

Large Nose
13 holes x 8 holes
Cut 1

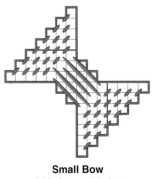

Small Bow
14 holes x 14 holes
Cut 2

The full line of The Needlecraft Shop
products is carried by Annie's Attic catalog.
TOLL-FREE ORDER LINE
or to request a free catalog
(800) 582-6643
Customer Service
(800) 449-0440
Visit AnniesAttic.com

We have made every effort to ensure the accuracy
and completeness of these instructions. We cannot,
however, be responsible for human error, typographical
mistakes or variations in individual work.

ISBN: 978-1-57367-338-9

Printed in USA

1 2 3 4 5 6 7 8 9

Shopping for Supplies

For supplies, first shop your local craft
and needlework stores. Some supplies
may be found in fabric, hardware and
discount stores. If you are unable to find
the supplies you need, please call Annie's
Attic at (800) 582-6643 to request a free
catalog that sells plastic canvas supplies.

Getting Started

Before You Cut

Buy one brand of canvas for each entire project as brands can differ slightly in the distance between bars. Count holes carefully from the graph before you cut, using the bolder lines that show each 10 holes. These 10-count lines begin in the lower left corner of each graph to make counting easier. Mark canvas before cutting; then remove all marks completely before stitching. If the piece is cut in a rectangular or square shape and is either not worked, or worked with only one color and one type of stitch, the graph is not included in the pattern. Instead, the cutting and stitching instructions are given in the general instructions or with the individual project instructions.

Covering the Canvas

Bring needle up from back of work, leaving a short length of yarn on back of canvas; work over short length to secure. To end a thread, weave needle and thread through the wrong side of your last few stitches; clip. Follow the numbers on the small graphs beside each stitch illustration; bring your needle up from the back of the work on odd numbers and down through the front of the work on even numbers. Work embroidery stitches last, after the canvas has been completely covered by the needlepoint stitches.

Basic Stitches

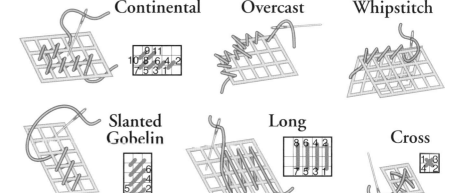

Continental   Overcast   Whipstitch

Slanted Gobelin   Long   Cross

Embroidery Stitches

French Knot

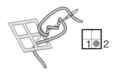

Lazy Daisy

Backstitch

Straight

METRIC KEY:
millimeters = (mm)
centimeters = (cm)
meters = (m)
grams = (g)